# The Rhino Narrative

Theodore Worozbyt

First Edition: 2023
Rs. 200/-

*Cyberwit.net*
HIG 45 Kaushambi Kunj, Kalindipuram
Allahabad - 211011 (U.P.) India
http://www.cyberwit.net
Tel: +(91) 9415091004
E-mail: info@cyberwit.net



Printed at VCORE.

# Contents

# I

# The Night

The light flew backwards from the streetlight in the back yard. It was eight. It stayed that way. Suppertime was over, not a shell steak that particular night cooked medium rare and basted in butter as was frequent by then, only Nutro Ultra. The light turned into the leaves it struck. The five oaks stood against the street impersonating always. I knew five things then. Four of them turned out wrongly. He went out, I followed, watching his thinned flanks rise and fall and hearing his cat-like pads tick down the ramp. He moved among the oak knees and looked at the street. I did not see this. He turned, to come inside. He started to come inside.

# Catkins

The warmth of the night fell with the catkins like gold even softer than gold. It was May, as if I might look up and detect the stars moving into some pattern, like a portrait gazing past my face to the left from the wall, just so.

# The Songs

On the radio someone said, No one listens to us, not anymore. Then I stepped through the screen, carrying him, the photograph of my hands not even real yet, just taped on a door, like a pair of spiders between a tree. The songs lay on the table, saturated with Technicolor covers. Each had an eye for itself. No one could listen to the smoke in their eyes. The photographer quipped: I am only making you hold him this long because I want to watch him get heavy. In your face, that is.

# The Caretaker

A portrait in coal dust hangs over me, not mine, slightly crooked under glass, not done by me, that I am referred to in the memory that follows its caretaker. The radio would not replace itself. Its green tube was slow to fade.

# Eight Spiders

I'm tired, his settled gaze seemed to say, almond eyes a brown study, his long whiskery jaw resting on my thigh as I sat on the john in another memory of watching a pheasant fly, all colors exceeding my vision. In my arms there was no one. There was no last idea of a moment. It was eight o'clock at night, then it was eight again but I could see the gray informing the sky that the night was done with the time it had had.

# Unforgivable

In the blanket only something resembling the cold pudding-like red mass behind the Chinese restaurant that remained flyless and undiscolored for weeks by the dumpster where I found the living mouse in the glue trap and came down with a cinder block. All three of us were there, man-father, dog-son, dun-colored mouse. In the mirror I can't say. I can't apologize but I did before I brought down the sky. I was sorry in a way I did not sort out. I slept alone there on the cloud in the living room so he wouldn't be alone. The next day there was an aroma like Socrates had gotten drunk.

# Baby and Fire

I rolled down the windows on the way to the firehouse so that I would not vomit the whiskey I scooped before I carried him. I paid with a card. The flames smelled of perfume, as if I myself were becoming a lie. I had stared at the opened black infinity hatch, and the lady who kept saying the word "baby" wondered aloudly whether I could lift his lightened weight alone. The man there, who took my card, used the same word twice as he swiped my card through the crack of invisible lightning in his machine.

# John

I carried him into the sound of the piped music playing itself like an instrument designed to undo music. I could not then imagine the way John Keats took a sequence of scalpels and bended those apple letters with his mind toward autumn's unbridling fetters. There was a man with two eyes bent. Each one held a newspaper to its lips and then disappeared in a scudding wrack, though there was no cloud to be seen and no this or that, if you please. The man on the radio said: I suppose the difference between regret and sorrow will always be that regret is over things you think you could have changed, while sorrow is what you knew all along you never could.

# Unspoken

But as to the question of "gret," he said. There was more, but I turned him off, sickened by his rhetoric. One sentence to each cell. Or fewer, now. Somewhere between those words, a long white water bird flaps out and comes to rest in the refrigerator where I keep only cans and bottles and the arms of certain putative galaxies. The box I clasped between my thighs grew cold in an hour. Since there was nothing else to do, I noticed it. And since, then, there was nothing left to do at all again but think about myself and how I would be from then on, I put it on the table.

# The Two-eyed Man

Nothing like dirty glass to make a room look like a dirty room, said the two-eyed man.

# Heaven

He lay on the needles fallen up the hill, tumbled and jerked like a fish pulled up to the grass, and his eye stared at me, wild and imploring. I remembered something better but just as wild as he looked at me, and said it aloud to him over and over, wishing we could disappear together into a path of brown studied needles where he walks ahead of me and I watch the metronome of his body sway that never ends.

# What I Tell You

There is something I am not telling you.

# Waves

The radio floated waves in a way. A beachball commenced rolling toward its own personal rainbow of infinity. A beauty with a mole and a white dog on the beach watch it disappear. They are not looking seaward. I had stopped by the catacombs and parted with my scalp, made and lost a music that was sleeping forever sleeping. In a week there wasn't one black hair in the basket of blankets and I have not found one still so I took them, the sole plurals of my nose following itself (what to ancient Greeks was *past* since one could see it) to the abandoned orphanage and caught a plane five miles above the summers of Radiohead Abbey, stumbled in Dublin's tows of Dover sole, and left for the airport in Apple-golden Vincent's Amsterdams, where Leonard Cohen wasn't ever truly expected in Warsaw and the frosty clouds slid on low arcs along the sky beneath my sun, my glyphic sun, where the swans were given permissions not to sing. "Did you forget a grey hat that wasn't, couldn't be yours? and pardon, which was to the Whisper Plain the way?" I asked of some doyenne much too kind for the likes of me, whose passport I pilfered and ground to flour in some ramshackle kitchen where the grease was sour and the pumpernickel stale and no whipped butter got left in the tub by the wooden-shoed Satan who had taken up residence between my crooked toes, as a grief takes up a life as its way. Forgive me. I am speaking out of turn.

# In Idaho

In a word: that nickeled hat which used to be mine and Stevie Ray
Vaughn's rode to Idaho on the taste of the wind. Why not? said what
hashish I chewed indifferently, in the provincial airport of a country
whose name, whose names, escape me, whose rivers are a map of
woven spiders in the pearlescent lights of the northern ends. I knew a
man, the radio said, quietly, who kept a tiger by his bed, but he always
kept a revolver in its cage, just so, in these cases.

# Star Trek

When, finally, after the tripe report and the how-to-farm-yourself segment, the news of the Eastern conflicts concluded itself, I set a timer on the two-eyed radio and vanished into my wife's elbow, which I cupped and kissed as she slept, gentling her tubercular cough of sympathies and symphonies and sinless sins, that I mix in my best dreams with a powder of skies and charcoals glowing in the pit; with these I predict false eternities on her plates of bone and gold. I pray to the slightly crooked tooth, snowy and bent toward the sky. Then I say goodnight to no one, aloud, and turn on the television with no sound. Mr. Spock's face seems redder than it should be; his blood is coppered.

# Well

I have to walk to the kitchen now, where the shadow of the bag still is, though my knees are broken into their fluids like hardtack, because I am thirsty for the water from the well, and the plantain when I get there is dark and unreadable, the jug not quite empty but still not enough. I remember that I will not be able to remember enough to make any of this complete. I only know what I am not saying.

# The Temperature of Love

Love is not a temperature, and other lies, read the covers of paperback books in Singapore, my antepenultimate stop, where I got my stripes for spitting into the mind of the wind. The cherry blossoms bend and turn to apples in Tokyo. My thanks go to geodes and nightmare gales. I'll be seeing you in all the now unfamiliar places. Dead butterflies are mounting up on the subspeaker, remaining bright, and presend the images and colorful sounds of flying. The Luna mouth that has no mouth, the tigertail swallowing its flight, seem a picture of music that isn't playing. I could start it up again, twirling my ouroboros with a lifting finger, as the piccolos meander.

# Just Me

The saw grass grew parted by the sea, his lips rose rippling in the rearview mirror in the wind, the sliver ascended toward his brain where roots grew, the sand growing whiter, whited, tilting like the hill of his brain toward the water. Under the arrow and incensed asleep, he took a tooth to bed and lost it, while all the poison regretted itself down Dr. Danica's drain. Listen to the liquids of his stumbling, smell how much cane we had in his coffee bones that long day in its hours! How the dust rolled soft as lizard necks down his shoulders and into the river fishing. None doubted, or so I tried to say. Not even Thomas knew then how to make a circle of himself around that unbecalmed afternoon of flames and clouds. A finger stabbed my chest but who could mind it, I was so much not wanting to say anothering other word, the word in the brain, an octet of shadows. How selfish to hoard the spiders in and identical to one's own hair.

# Glyphic

I left them in the slate-colored light on a tethered boat where some spiders wore invisible shoes and braces and waltzed furiously among their lines. "Shall we leave this for little Anna to find?" said the warped face in the plank on the floor of the deck as you turned your palm toward the sink, and the colors of the crayons on the cabin walls grew steadily brighter until I could not keep my eyes open and by closing them let everything else in: the falling through a corkscrew light, the slipping in between what wasn't, the helpers in the corners that flattened or got bigger. I was floating between some of my recently abrogated finger bones and cigarettes, and what is white water in the swans if not the same air where clouds pretend to be swans shaped like platinum thunder? The deep black imagination of the glyph, the bird at the window seemed to say, golden and silent and nothing if not a serene imago of herself, not looking at me but there, in me suddenly, reckoning me among the cooled and humming stars. I found that I was weeping, weeping in a sweeping enfold of the you that entered the undulating room. I seem to be weeping, I said. Why not? you cheerily replied. Come with me, I am going where the dogs go!

# The Weight of Nothing

He weighed precisely nothing, just like a soul being happy as it can be, dancing in one ossuary after another, musical, ambulatory, vibrating like this McClintock clock counting seconds less quickly than the blue-eyed Chinese chef in Canada we finally stopped watching. A pump organ raises dust in some nearby room where the best Dickens novel (*Bleak House,* according to dead Kenneth Payne, dead of HIV, a skull fracture from crossing the street in front of an uninsured motorist employed by 7-11, complications from gangrene requiring various amputations, and some final thing I cannot discover) in a first edition stands rebound, half-bound in camel leather, its value lessened but its beauty increased, something not to read but to cherish, like the moss and wood beetles of some afternoon only one of you, the only one of you, will recognize.

# Undated Sunday

The day I learned most about rain we were in Tuscaloosa, where Baudelaire thought in offal, and in our walk we were farthest from home, at the Medical Field. It was not a Thursday in the rain as for Vallejo but it was a Sunday as it was for everyone who was not on the empty streets so there was no leashing, and we walked unmolested along the sidewalks smelling the things on the ground or looking into the evenly spaced oak trees or at the unburned buildings of the university on the boulevard as the light changed on them from pearl to the gray of rubber crutch handles and then became much darker. It was as dark as a tornado coming but there was not the feeling of the air becoming thin and suffused with the cordite smell and there was not the strange swelling of the light, and then there was no horn, nor any tornado with actual horns that were made of smaller tornadoes rising from the sides of a column roaring so much louder than the sea and like a dark avalanche pursuing itself down the boulevard eating every tree and wall and window where cameras pointed their apertures; that would come much later, after we had packed our swollen arms and bags and bumping over curbs had gone, so I knew it was only going to be rain.

# II

# In Egypt

Someone broke your jaw in Egypt and someone else faked your death in Saipan, said the reports I'd read and sent. Changing Seikos in front of a wavy mirror, I knew none of it could stay true. The electrodes in their unstamped envelope of twenty-dollar bills don't add up to a reduction in the swelling of the waves in your brain, said Art, who claimed he wasn't raised that way. I didn't even know about that yet that summer when your head hung out the window and your jaw dripped along the carpet and the foam. I never knew we could have this conversation, even here. I wish what you thought that day would roll to me like a watch winder's grinding wave.

# Two

There were two large shells that I fell above my broken bones and dived for.  Only one came home, and only I remember the other one now. It isn't worth disturbing the surface of my home to ask about it twice. Meanwhile the cardinal cocks his gaze to the tiny, glossy snail involutions that position themselves like a history in the making on the white top of a tiny computer. In that same city by the gulf there is a book my wife writes in with a dog claw in her left hand. She isn't left-handed; only she and the universe think she is.

# Shells

I sewed the foam up with the swellings in my tendons and fell headfirst into the water, like a mouse smelling a pear in the gloaming. (Who but you will ever know what that means?) I slipped in, where the outgoing undulations of bone were not clear, and floated along the edges, hungry and thirsty in the water. I could not lift her in the sharkstream or carry her into the house where the jewelfish are live. I could not stand in the water, a simple fact. The sands were moving with the waves. I took a strand of beige grass and stitched it around my jaw and said the words of love that are the remains within me. I love your white shadow, who does not care for the ocean. I love these shrimp, and how you eat them with your shell steak.

# Not Even a Question

Richard Yates should have had the steak at Red Lobster, I thought, as we walked past the ceremonial row of tiny brick houses where he kept the Bob Kennedy manuscript in the freezer. You needed a key from the landlord to get that, and there was none. When Bobby was shot I was on the floor. What was I doing, you might ask, but why would you. It's not even a question at this point. I sat on the floor in front of the leopard skin chaise lounge and watched cartoons. When William F. Buckley came into the room with my mother-to-been I looked at them funny and said it, that Bobby Kennedy was shot. I said it so matter of factly that they didn't believe a word, but they did soon enough, and there was that strange crying thought me, the very abstracted child who could only remember best a glove lying on the floor in a dream that came true, but had no meaning.

# The Bush of Many Species

Where the rain was a school the yard was a side more than a front and when you were young you needed no restraints, but there was the summer day when I pushed past you cutting the grass and saw that as you lay in the cool shoal beside the bush of many species by the window where the ladders hid you had changed in the minute I'd been gone.

# Formic

That spot of crimson on the fence just now was a leaf, not a cardinal....
In the kitchen where the laundry is turning the ants resemble nothing so
much in their orderly rings around the cotton balls soaked in caster
sugar syrup and borax as tiny, tiny piglets suckling a sow. You were
lumpy. That's what I saw, and then that your skin was moving. Skin
doesn't crawl, ants do, so the phrase lies backwards, and the fiery ants
were biting and you did not care enough about whatever pain meant to
you to lift yourself and move.

# Absurd Naming

Certain mushrooms grow only in shadow, and in Belgium Belgian endive is called chicory. And there's another name for it, growing in shadow. The houses where I mention your name look like the same houses we spelt in, but the architecture and upkeep and multiple professional appliances are all quite different: white noise in every room, a tiny screen glowing, and when your name is mentioned: silence, or something louder but even more silently obscured. Let's seem taller, or be the little sweet one with a high voice, as we run through the grass to the creek without a dog. I repeat, without a dog. And the logic needed to place the bowls where they would be needed? Sorry. No go. Peekaboo! Chinquapin! Stickaman! Every litany a tumble of syllables old as the round stones in the mouth of the stream.

# Not Home

I felt quite at home with the baby, more so at a slight distance, though as time passes she allows that distance less. Perhaps this baby will resuscitate me after all, lull me from my sleep sack and yell the almost words you would have understood far better than I, never having lost that affect, as the long-gone doctor said. Good old Dr. Danica, who got on her knees on the floor and ripped that thing from your face. I wished it were the roots of the other thing inside.

# Alors

(The distorted egg rock that weights the tin lid that holds his leftover bits in a tin box has a skin that was once unbroken; its surface still mimics what the maps didn't look like because there were no maps. Everything was closer together and the need for them didn't exist yet. Now its skin is moon-colored and observed closely seems to resemble far away. Just under that runs the ring of black that killed the friendly brontosaurus. As we move in, please, to spectate the impending diorama there are colors, the colors of agates common in North Dakota as well as South, but at the center there is no hollow, only more cleaved mineral. And that's the end of that brief tour, alors. )

# Australia

I can't imagine what broke it so cleanly, leaving not a trace of the fracture along its tableau. Most of it remains. One might say the very best part, since now we see inside with magnets. I only know that I looked down as his blackly brindled legs bunched like Bresse chooks and flew him away down the field and its suddenly eternal passway of starry yellow flowers. I looked down and picked it up, that rock. My air cast was blue and so was the sky around my ankles. Sydney saw him and said, He looked so happy to be there. Rhino, I said, is happy to be anywhere.

# Both Here and There

I put it in my pocket on another day and glanced through a camera at the sky. What remained were the blossoms of the mimosa tree, and the fingers of the nervured leaves. The millipede lies resting along my tensed and untensed knee. The ants are parading in the kitchen, the cocklebug whirls in the downtown of the toilet. Every day I sit with my back against the wall and no chair under me, as long as I can. The cardinal with no legs drops forward perched on the apple drive as if to peck, but instead regards something I can't see, but I feel as though I am seeing it.

# Left

Every bone in my more sinister leg is broken, and there's a paper cut dripping in my eye. My heart has four chambers. Its action is amazingly accurate and smooth. My digression has five bulls. I want some kind of sixties oil to burble in my chest of compartments and drawers. It seems a matter of refinements rather than purposes to do this job I am doing. Therefore I'm driving right past its exit and continuing to the town that is as next as I want it.

# Not Rhino

I chewed the slow horse teeth from the last corn of the year at my dinner, and stung myself with green as radium on the dial. I will never have run again. Australia starts up, in another year. My old GP warred itself to sleep and stopped the day along my wrist but the date is some forgotten day now. I almost called you in, though by now who "you" is is anyone's guess, at least until next time. The way was woozy in the driveway from the bed through the hatch and the red door where the salamander twitched slowly under a rock under the rain. I jumped off the wall, never to be seen inside myself again.

# You

There wasn't much you liked about the rain until the day on the powerline red with clay and dust, when down past the deerberries in the buzzing-tower sun you ran to the bottom of the hill into the green and leapt, leapt into one long, slow leap into leaping into the air, leaving your body into the green sinkpond that did not seem a pond because no water was visible, only green, like money or nasturtium leaves on the surface of the space between the earth and the moon or a droplet on my eye and past it you plunged like a frog through lilies, and came up green as the emeralds hiding in the ring that is hiding in this house. You swam in the sun, and green then was your Echo, green the black gloss of his sister, rising from that hollowed mud.

# Bezel

A ruffed grouse rose dust in the air, and the scarlet paint that ringed the oaks was fresh. We had hoped it was only the late light that made it seem so. I smoked then. What a strange thing, in the aftermath, to have smoked. What is called feeling? is the question we must ask myself today. But lest I run and jump upon the query and in so doing crush my heel—not as Achilles in some enduring hubris and hybris of myth or perhaps a myth thereof, nor even upon the viper's head as its fang sinks its way into my bones—but just crush it, like a rotten and infested log that into red powder falls in slow time of its own accord, and watch myself collapse into nowhere, I counsel myself (Who else will counsel me now? In these years? I put my hand upon a chair. Something I meant to do in this room, or that one, seems almost accomplished, almost done…) to feel nothing, to feel nothing at all. The stone I found today at the top of a hill was once in a river. Though now the sun streams through it pinkly and whitely, occluded and round. The crystals in her watch are oiled, the diamonds on its bezel break sonnetas in the light. I see in you my stream of time undone. Wait, wait. But there is no waiting, and Apple has run so deeply into the woods that I cannot see him, as he does every day, as you never did, and now I am the one waiting, just as I supposed I always was.

# Today a Man Fell Out of the Sky

Today a man fell out of the sky and landed on the sidewalk in front of my wife. Pink beans, she said, long after screaming, and things tinged yellow, much smaller than you'd think, and everyone then got locked into my Suntrust bank. Then she walked away when the police came. Who can blame her. They say he was on the sidewalk for an hour before they sheeted him, and it was dinnertime before they were done. Some posted videos and jokes on the threads that weave our collections of consciousness into the record books. In her dream she sees herself in the building, being dragged along for the fall. In her dream she puts a gun to his face and pulls the trigger. His red shirt was the only truly red thing in a blue, sunny sky. I tell her that he must have worn it just that way. The president released a message. His parents were rumored on the apps. The basement was not open to his gardens of withered gradations. I tell her you were never weak, but I do not speak of the way your eye looked at me when the lesion threw you to the ground in the pine wood where I have never once been able to dream the dream I wish for, the one of you walking before me on the path of pine needles, your spine undulating, hips crab-swaying, ears gathered but still flopping, trotting like a light fish on a sparkling wave, as we walk into the sunlight and do not stop walking. I do not tell her what I know about that day.

# Game

I like to think that you would not have insisted on ripping out Apple's throat or underbelly, even though Miko and Bluebaby and all the rest of the neighborhood cats are his friends, not like that white puffed flat-faced ninja-kitty that sailed one summer Tuscaloosa afternoon from the rectangly manicured bushes onto your back where you slunk along the shadowed sidewalk, sinking in her claws.

# Albino Rhino

The map on his face doesn't say the fourth of July, but has a patch of oath to it, a little rascal wallpaper reminder in the oatmeals of steel cut mornings, a smartness that even when photographed starving says something quizzical. In the distance I could see the sweaty fat man waving his arms in front of the factory's ruins. If it were Roswell Falls I could have explained myself. I once crawled and crossed the river ice of a frozen yet forgotten Sunday, and discovered that the falls were made for the mill, and that the mill turned the wheel, and that the wheel made the power, and that the power moved the looms, and the looms wove the cloth, and the cloth made that cloud color, in confederation. But this was another river, wider, there were other clouds filled with black dogs. I said to myself, If only there were *five* box turtles in a row I could be sure. And before I turned around there they came, box turtles in a row if not a tower, figured bright with strokes of canary, and still I was not sure.

# The Barrier of Symbols

In the counterstory is a way of identification, but not the only way, nor the only counterstory, just another color that will unspool a thread of ashes like the one with an agate hat just starboard of my elbow in the marbly pink light. As this happens he lies near, poised on the symbols in the Hamadan rugs, but when I think of him he gets up to go into the other room, to sleep where I lie when I sleep.

# Time is Not a Flavor

I have not read where the schedule ends. It ended sooner than I expected. My robe was rented and lacked a hood. Something seemed too familiar in the music. Let's just say I felt as though I had never felt it before. That is not what I meant. I placed the speakers in the wrong places. The palace of wisdom is duller on my tongue. So I bought Stilton. To correct my stilted speeches. To taste stillness. Stilliness. I have promised to sleep in my bed tonight, not in the place not far from it. A door slaps shut.

# III

# First Tick

That tick gleamed oxblood on his black snout, which had always borne a salivary rope crackling across its cavities and which no scrub of my nails could completely dislodge, not even in the bath, a desiccated biological materiel that coated his short snout fur and the windows and portraits and the cloths that I used to moisten the crusts on his lips and loins, the skin thin as living vellum on his thighs, fish belly pale, the pawnails just long as finishing brads, but thicker. A handful of rice meal and lamb bones shaped like a bone; that was a first taste of liver on a rock, that tick the exact color of bird liver, like these shoes and the echoes of these shoes that make the same sounds in the woods as everything moving. You know which bird.

# Fired

Before or after that, the desiccated lizard held so lightly in the tweezers; he snapped it shut in his jaw, the bolus of muscle barely moving. Yum yum. There was no end to how funny he was. I stood in the walk-in. I never felt cold enough where the ducks and snails were stacked and I hid. After I smashed the Hobart onto the ground and broke its galvanized neck, Bob Mazurek bought a new one, giant and caged to keep the flours from making clouds. I split a gallon of hollandaise and drinkingly hissed at the cappuccino machine, and dreamt nightly of the fresh flowers in the ladies room that Carmen had chosen herself and put there herself while Cao the cleaning man stole and wore my Florsheim dress shoes to clean the toilets every morning. Those flavors were wrapped in squared steel. They turned out to be Noilly Prat and nutmeg, is my best guess now, that and the taste of endless days as well as the hot clarified butter smell of the ends of my days, when service had just started, and there was nothing, I thought then, lonelier than that, walking out the back door at twilight with all the stocks and sauces done and the veg cut, and the bread baked, the twists and rolls and salt sticks and ryes and pumpernickels, to catch the 23 into town to the trains and home.

# The Geode

A black diamond, with an inclusion of the air underneath the world. A white diamond, with a black bow tie in its center. Accidental images of the soul in its own fixtures. The rooms had been emptied of their period furniture. The hardwood floors were scraped and grooved but had a chestnut depth that caught the sun falling through the tall window. The row of windows was high off the floor and reached almost to the ceiling of the loft, out of which everything had been dragged but into which had been pulled on a blanket the corpse of a wolf. It lay on the blanket with its head turned toward the wind, tongue out, eyes filmed.

Its eyes were filmed over with white and its white fur was stiff except for the fur thin on the belly where the ticks would climb and behind the ears where the fleas rushed up from the underside of the neck and into the canals of the ears instead of drowning.

In the long room where he lay on the blanket my wife and I looked down and I saw the first of the ants crawl out. They were carpenter ants. She touched his haunch with her bare foot and then they flooded out and by the time we reached the other room they had formed masses in circular mounds here and there. Then they grew apart from the humming mounds and the first of the grasshoppers stepped on their stalk legs away from the caviar of ants. The grasshoppers grew larger than kangas; they weren't the brown hoppers that spit tobacco juice on your fingers. They were the shiny black ones banded with orange stripes or yellow so that they looked and flew like the sun.

What was left was to go back. We went there. The room was still. There was nothing we wanted to say. We said nothing. I seemed then to have no expectations; except to find something there. On the blanket was a husk of crisp skin covered with fur and no bones. There was nothing inside left. When I started to pull the blanket across the floor the husk broke in two like a dull geode.

# Describing Figures

The music is not as I recall it, none of it. The equipment I replaced was the same, except for the letters of the name embossed into the cabinet of the sub bass system on the slabs. And yet. The umbrella from the opera was lost in the rain, the rain across which Isabelle Faust once again draws the partita of her bow, as though no one had noticed the words lying there in rows like strangers in hospital beds, their curtains drawn but the silver light from their phones visible through the curtains. None look at their curtains. A study conducted by no one concludes that the world isn't the same. And who knows, everything may turn out that way. Seeking in it is like the music I can't quite listen to because it sounds less and less like the way I remember it. Even now. I mean right now. Like there's nothing between us here.

# Verjus

The bad way to die would be of a lingering disease. I have had two now. Most people dream of spiders as nightmares. The night I found a wolf spider in my hair I looked in the mirror over the sink and noticed that my hair was moving. I carried him in my hand to the door. That was not a dream. In the dream last night the wolf spider was toad-sized, a color he shares. He crawled over the hot water faucet in the kitchen, where the water from the heater I have adjusted is much too hot. I tried to watch his progress but he disappeared. In Australia the spiders are large as dinner plates and crawl up the sides of refrigerators like crabs but no one eats them. Instead they eat Balmain bugs, and barra, and all the things they eat with verjus.

# More Names

The first got called Reiter's Syndrome, and it is called something else now, because Reiter was a Nazi and people remembered later. Nisbet Toole cured me by telling me to wait it out. The second was consumption. I like to call it consumption because of Hemingway and I have eaten tournedos with Chateau Neuf Du Pape. I also prefer to say TB instead of its longer name: Richard Yates. There is nothing Keatsian about tuberculosis, if you know what I mean. Exactly when Fortunato started coughing is not in the end a literary question. Everything rimes eventually. Everything rhymes eventually.

# Just Like That

I lodged the brown heater cube between the wall and my pillows and at the foot of the bed the window showed the bush that was many plants growing through an original bush and the red birds would light there and peck on the sill looking into my room where I lay on the bed smoking when I used to smoke. It was winter. I turned the heater on the high setting and it blew red dark air along the wall toward the window where the wind whistled and rattled the sashes and the streetlight through the rolled glass panes passed through the bubbles in the glass. In the night when I would fall asleep at last he would rise in the dark and his legs as you can see in the picture on the river were like tall reflections in the water and he would slowly revolve and then without any reason or warning fall over. He would fall just like that and without any buckling just like a tree when the axe has felled it and his shoulder would hit my chest almost in the center and knock the breath out of me and quite naturally wake me from my sleep.

# Sun

I think now that getting old and dying is not frightening. I imagine getting more and more tired until I fall asleep and do not wake up, so that death becomes a sleep that comes after a dream or after a number of dreams that all tangle together into a fabric that is like the blanket I sleep under; light, soft, and warm. The one we bought this year was white. It is not so soft yet as the first, but now our dog is white, too, and his dreams are of lighthouses because we found him inside one, all alone, his knee broken, in a lighthouse that looked like a powerline, and a powerline that looked like an artery of clay, dried in another summer's sun.

# Acknowledgements

*The National Poetry Review*: "The Geode"

*Otoliths*: "Albino Rhino" and "Sun"

www.ingramcontent.com/pod-product-compliance
Lightning Source LLC
Chambersburg PA
CBHW060506160726
47992CB00003B/1363